CRAFTS
OF THE MIDDLE AGES™

THE CRAFTS AND CULTURE OF A
MEDIEVAL CATHEDRAL

Joann Jovinelly and Jason Netelkos

The Rosen Publishing Group, Inc., New York

For Mom, a spirited and creative woman who taught me it was possible to make magic

Published in 2007 by The Rosen Publishing Group, Inc.
29 East 21st Street, New York, NY 10010

Library of Congress Cataloging-in-Publication Data

Jovinelly, Joann.
The crafts and culture of a medieval cathedral/Joann Jovinelly and Jason Netelkos.—1st ed.
    p. cm.—(Crafts of the Middle Ages)
Includes index.
ISBN 1-4042-0758-9 (library binding)
1. Handicraft—Europe—History—To 1500—Juvenile literature. 2. Cathedrals—Europe—
History—To 1500—Juvenile literature. 3. Middle Ages—Europe—History—Juvenile literature.
I. Netelkos, Jason. II. Title. III. Series: Jovinelly, Joann. Crafts and culture of the Middle Ages.
TT55.J6725 2006
726.6094'0902—dc22

2005034041

Manufactured in the United States of America

Note to Parents
Some of these projects require tools or materials that can be dangerous if used improperly. Adult supervision will be necessary when projects require the use of a craft knife, an oven, cut aluminum, or pins and needles. Before starting any of the projects in this book, you may want to cover your work area with newspaper or plastic. In addition, we recommend using a piece of thick cardboard to protect surfaces while cutting with craft or mat knives. We encourage you to discuss safety with your children and note in advance which projects may require your supervision.

CONTENTS

Cathedrals are some of the most impressive structures from the Middle Ages, the period after the fall of the Roman Empire in AD 476 and before the Renaissance in the fifteenth century. They are breathtaking monuments of ingenuity, long-standing testaments to Christianity. Unlike churches, which could be found in towns, cathedrals were located in cities and were the home of the bishop's *kathedra*, a Greek word that means "seat." The region over which a bishop ruled was called a diocese, and it was made up of smaller churches. The largest cities had an archbishop in the cathedral who oversaw the bishops. The bishops presided over local priests, and all of these holy men gave spiritual direction to the Christians who populated the area.

Before cathedrals were built throughout western Europe, however, years of hardship had gripped the region following the Roman period. Germanic outsiders had invaded the empire from all points. These "barbarians"—Goths, Franks, Lombards, Vandals, Angles, and Saxons—would eventually form kingdoms of their own, all of them competing for power.

Notre Dame Cathedral is seen at sunset from across the Seine River in this photograph. The building of Notre Dame began in 1163 under the direction of Maurice de Sully, bishop of Paris. It took roughly 180 years to complete.

Towns and cities were formed where these groups settled. Castle and cathedral building experienced its height in the eleventh and twelfth centuries after western Europe had begun to stabilize.

Cathedral building allowed the participation of every member of medieval society. This included everyone from the architects and stonemasons who designed and built cathedrals to the bishops and deacons who counseled their worshippers. Even the poorest of peasants contributed money to the

This map of Europe shows the approximate reach of Christianity between 600 and 1300, the height of the Middle Ages. Christianity and Islam were the predominate religions of the medieval period.

church in support of cathedral construction. When they could not give money, they donated grain to help feed hungry workers.

Erecting even the simplest cathedral took years and generations of laborers. At the height of the Middle Ages, England and France were home to thousands of cathedrals and churches.

THE FIRST CATHEDRALS

The first cathedrals were built in the Romanesque style, named after the Romans, whose tastes they depicted. Romanesque cathedrals, popular from about 900 to 1200, had thick walls, rounded doors, and rounded arches supported by arcades, or row of columns.

Barrel vaults, semicircular masonry roofs that stood atop columns, supported the ceilings. Vaulted ceilings had originated in Roman basilicas, which were long, rectangular buildings with one rounded eastern end. Basilicas were originally courts of law in ancient Greece and Rome. They had been erected in Rome since 184 BC, but by the fourth century AD, their rounded design was used exclusively for churches. Christians adapted this design and utilized the rounded basilica, which they renamed the apse, as a place from which Christian leaders spoke to followers.

Romanesque cathedrals therefore began with some elements common to Roman buildings. But cathedrals soon developed specific architectural details. One element common to cathedrals was that the altar needed to face east, toward the rising sun. Seeing the rising sun each day represented the resurrection of Jesus Christ, an important event for Christians. Another architectural consideration was that a cathedral represent the holy cross, or take on a cruciform (cross-shaped) design.

In England, Romanesque cathedrals were built in abundance after the Norman conquest of the region in 1066. Among the most impressive of all of the Norman constructions is Durham Cathedral in northern England near the Scottish border. Because Durham Cathedral sits naturally on a peninsula, it also made an excellent fortress. Durham Cathedral combined Romanesque elements with newly styled cross-rib vaults, a style that would later be used in Gothic cathedrals.

Because Romanesque cathedral ceilings required the support of such thick walls, their windows were slender and did not allow much light inside. Romanesque cathedrals were typically dark, open structures, with columns flanking the nave (the main east-west interior of a cathedral). They were generally somber. Besides being a necessity, it is also thought that this style was intentional. Darkness emphasized the mystery of Mass and of Christianity. As time went on, however, Romanesque builders mastered the vaulting technique. They increased the height of cathedrals using new combinations of vaults and arches. The cathedral at Cluny, in France, for example, was rebuilt in 1088 and rose to a height of 98 feet (30 meters). As the naves rose higher, the intricacies of cathedral architecture also developed. It was now possible to add rows of windows to brighten cathedral interiors. Natural light was preferable for a variety of reasons, mostly because it represented the true light of God. Using candlelight or lamplight in the form of hanging lamps was risky, caused a lot of smoke, and provided little illumination. Christian popes had for years been urging builders to hire artists to paint scriptural scenes on interior walls for the benefit of illiterate parishioners. These scenes were difficult to see with such little light. The race continued to construct a cathedral with larger windows, especially as people sought to celebrate and glorify God.

GOTHIC INFLUENCES

Over time, architectural advancements continued and various types of arches were developed. These included the pointed (ogival) arch, the rib or cross-rib vault, and the flying buttress. Natural light was always a consideration. Larger windows caused supporting arches to be raised above the aisle roofs to meet the vaults. Since this design made the supporting arches appear to be "flying" over the vaults on the exterior of the building, they were named flying buttresses. The flying buttress design shifted the weight of the roof and vaults to side structures. This allowed cathedrals to be built larger and taller. More natural light could now fill the interior nave since the thick walls once necessary to support the roof were no longer needed.

These combinations of pointed arches, ribbed and crossed vaults, and flying buttresses became hallmarks of Gothic architecture. Pointed arches were more versatile than rounded arches. Because they were narrower and able to support more weight, Gothic cathedrals became tall, imposing structures complete with towering spires. Tall, narrow windows called lancets, doorways, and arcades all took the pointed arch design, and the results were revolutionary. Gothic designs quickly spread throughout western Europe and, over time, many Romanesque cathedrals were updated to reflect the new style. Notre Dame Cathedral in Paris is an exquisite example of a Gothic cathedral, as are the Cathedral of Chartres and England's Salisbury Cathedral, which also features the world's tallest spire, rising to 404 feet (123 meters).

This image of the Cathedral of Pisa, built from 1067 to 1173, shows its interior nave and basilica. The rounded design of the interior and arches are characteristic of the Romanesque style in which it was built.

Other parts of Gothic cathedrals included the huge, recessed doorways. Above each was the tympanum, which was usually filled with intricate carvings. Since visitors were made to feel as if they themselves were ascending to heaven, spires and finials (decorative spirelike accents) often appeared on top of buttresses. The apse at the end of the nave contained the altar and the choir. Several chapels were found within the nave and transept, and these were usually dedicated to various saints. Other parts of the cathedral complex included the chapter house (conference rooms), the cloister (open-air walkway), and a campanile (bell tower). Most cathedrals also had a crypt underneath the building where tombs, effigies, and treasures were housed.

The first wave of Gothic cathedral building began in the twelfth century. The style was inspired by the church of St. Denis, a monastery in Paris where French royalty was buried. St. Denis was the patron saint of France, considered "after God, [the] unique protector of the realm," and the church was home to his relics. Abbot Suger, who ruled over the abbey, resided there from 1122 to his death in 1151. During his tenure, France was made up of politically unstable feudal states. But Abbot Suger was the adviser to several successive French kings, one of whom he incited to unleash his French armies to subdue the German monarchy. Suger, who firmly believed that St. Denis would protect all who fought for France, bolstered support for French unification to keep the Germans at bay. He, along with French leaders, urged the support of the royal Abbey of St. Denis, even more so after the German rebels were overcome.

In return for his thanks to St. Denis for answering his prayers, the king ordered lavish gifts given to the abbey in the saint's honor. He urged a redesign of the abbey church. In an effort to re-create the church in a way that would do justice to its holy relics, Suger set out to change its style.

Suger had seen Gothic details such as ribbed vaults used in cathedrals in northern France. Ignoring Romanesque traditions, he envisioned a church with pointed arches, ribbed vaulting, enormous windows, and majestic vertical lines that soared toward heaven. The results were dramatic. The project began in 1135, and it took nine years to complete. Visitors to the redesigned Abbey Church of St. Denis in 1144 were in awe. Suger's vision then inspired all of western Europe to embrace Gothic architecture.

The flying buttresses of York Minster in North Yorkshire, England, are pictured in this photograph. York Minster is England's largest Gothic cathedral, dating back to the thirteenth century. Its flying buttresses allow it to rise to a height of more than 234 feet (71 meters).

THE CATHEDRAL BUILDERS

Once the Gothic style had taken hold, the race was on to rebuild some of the dated Romanesque cathedrals or to raze them completely. For the next 400 years, cathedrals all over Europe would be remade in the Gothic style. According to some historians, Abbot Suger's guest list to the opening of the Abbey Church of St. Denis was virtually the exact group of bishops whose cathedrals were redesigned in the years that followed.

The desire to create these Gothic cathedrals took enormous raw materials, tremendous skill and craftsmanship, and a keen sense of organization. The costs of completing a cathedral were staggering. By today's standards, estimates Robert A. Scott, author of *The Gothic Enterprise*, building a cathedral to match the size and workmanship of those constructed during the Middle Ages would range in "the hundreds of millions of dollars."

Even so, the costs of construction do not compare to the sheer number of obstacles involved during the process. Breaks in the flow of production were common. Outbreaks of disease, famine, civil unrest, shortages of materials and money, deaths on the job, and even losses due to collapse all played a part. In 1282, the choir of Beauvais Cathedral, the tallest Gothic cathedral ever built in France, collapsed. In fact, historians estimate that nearly 17 percent of all cathedrals and churches built during the Middle Ages collapsed during construction! Others were destroyed by fire and rebuilt, such as France's Chartres Cathedral. In more common occurrences, poor weather and lack of funds were very often the reasons construction ceased. Many times, this situation left the job at a point where a portion would have to be torn down and rebuilt when work commenced.

Despite their fragility, cathedrals remain among Western civilization's most impressive accomplishments. These awesome structures took, on average, 250 to 300 years each to complete. The magnitude of the achievement was even greater considering that the majority of workers who carried the stone blocks on thin scaffolding could not read or understand the mathematics useful for construction. Stonemasons, however, did need to understand practical geometry.

Once a design was set and the funds were raised, a site was chosen for the cathedral. Trenches were dug where its foundation was to be laid. Materials such as flint, which was available in England, were mixed with chunks of gravel and straw and poured into the trenches. Once the foundation dried completely, construction could begin. This always took place from east to west. Walls and pillars were assembled in stone with the addition of lime mortar. Once combined with water, the lime mortar reacted with the carbon dioxide in the air and hardened. Sometimes, depending on the humidity and weather, the mortar could take a few years to dry before vaulting could begin.

Assembling the stone was among the most difficult and costliest tasks. Because the stone was too heavy to be carried long distances over land, it was often shipped by sea. The stone that was used to build Canterbury Cathedral, for example, was shipped across the English Channel from Normandy. In other cases, sites were chosen that were within a reasonable distance from a quarry. Raising the stones to the top of a cathedral was also difficult. Materials were hoisted by rope, which workers coiled with the help of a large wheel called a windlass.

Most skilled workers on the site, usually between 100 to 200 men, probably came from far away. They were travelers in search of work. Unskilled laborers were paid poorly and had few benefits, unlike other workers who were provided with sleeping quarters and occasional meals. Work began at sunrise and ended at sunset. The medieval workweek averaged just four or five days, considering all of the Christian holidays. (Also, this workweek took place only in the spring and summer. Winter was spent carving stone.) Unskilled laborers had the hardest job because they had to transport stone without it chipping. Most stones were finished on one side only; each either had a facing interior or exterior side. In the middle between the two finished sides, laborers poured a mixture of mortar and rubble, which made up the cathedral's core. Using scrap materials helped control costs.

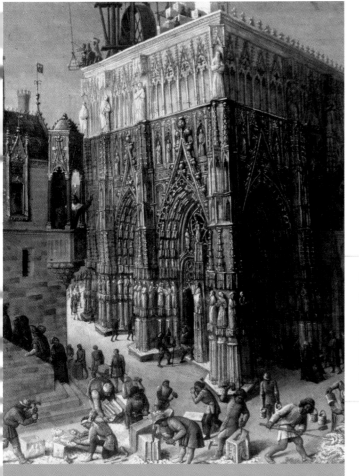

THE END OF AN ERA

The bubonic plague ravaged Europe toward the end of the cathedral period. Death eliminated many of the master cathedral builders. The effect of the plague on Gothic styles was dramatic, too. In England, the newer, less ornate carvings of the period between 1350 and 1450 were called perpendicular. The styles were more uniform, and much of the detailed carving was missing. Cathedrals of this era have massive windows, usually with many vertical divisions. The perpendicular style is mostly found in renovations of existing structures such as England's Winchester Cathedral. The zenith of great cathedral building had passed.

Certainly, the accomplishments of medieval architects cannot be overstated. Cathedrals are today one of the most alluring aspects of European architecture. Each one is a unique testament to its architects, master builders and masons, workers, and worshippers.

Cathedral builders work diligently in this fifteenth-century manuscript illumination. Most cathedrals took several centuries to build, with nearly half of that time marked by disruption due to lack of funds, war, and famines and epidemics.

Life in a Cathedral

As previously mentioned, a bishop was a person who was the head of his Christian diocese. He looked after all the churches in his region. Bishops did not care for cathedrals directly, however. He left those jobs to deacons, who were in charge of a group of clergy called canons. Together, the canons were known as a chapter, and they helped lead Christian services in the cathedral. This is why nearly every cathedral has a chapter house, a room where cathedral business is conducted, much like the chapter house in a monastery.

Because cathedrals were features of the cities in which they were built, there were plenty of decisions that had to be made by the canons. Besides daily Mass, cathedrals held baptisms, weddings, and funerals; were the sites of many religious festivals and saints' day celebrations; and often hosted weekly marketplaces in the city. For example, it was not uncommon during medieval

The archbishop (left) in this medieval manuscript illumination offers Communion to five newly ordained priests who kneel before him in front of a cross-bearer and two deacons. A chaplain holds the cup for purifying the communicants.

times to enter the nave of a cathedral and find merchants selling their wares and food. (If merchants were permitted a chance to sell goods inside the cathedral, they usually took the opportunity, since it was a sanctuary where profits could be made without being taxed.) In extreme cases, such as during outbreaks of disease, cathedrals sometimes

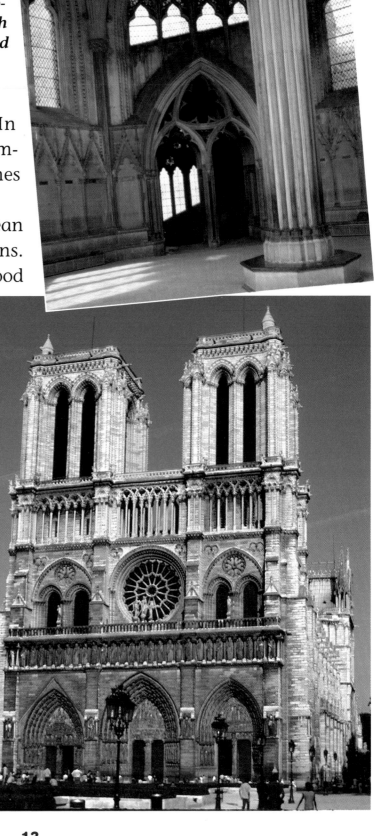

The chapter house of England's Wells Cathedral, with its Gothic ribbed vault construction, is the focus of this photograph. Finished in the mid-thirteenth century, Wells Cathedral is considered England's first fully Gothic cathedral.

became makeshift infirmaries. In general, the cathedral served its community in times of plenty and in times of poverty.

Workers were needed to help clean the cathedral and its possessions. Windows had to be washed, and wood had to be oiled. Metals were polished to a high sheen, especially the chalices and other items used during Mass. A priest's vestments (garments) had to be washed. Ornate carvings had to be dusted and polished. Many people helped serve their community by working in the cathedral and, in so doing, helped serve God.

The west front facade of France's Notre Dame Cathedral shows the beauty of its two towers and the Gothic design of its pointed arches. Built between the twelfth and thirteenth centuries, it was among the first cathedrals to feature flying buttresses that substantially increased its height.

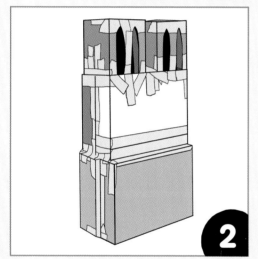

Cathedral Model

Create this example of a Gothic cathedral, complete with lancet windows and pointed arched doorways.

YOU WILL NEED
- 4 similarly sized cereal boxes
- large (1 lb.) cracker box
- Scrap cardboard
- Masking tape
- Glue
- Ruler and pencil
- Craft knife
- Scissors
- Compass
- Black felt-tip marker
- Paint
- Paintbrushes and sponge
- Bowl, glue/water mixture, and paper strips (for papier-mâché)

Step 1
Cut cracker box in equal halves with a craft knife. Using scissors, cut two long archways in each half, as shown.

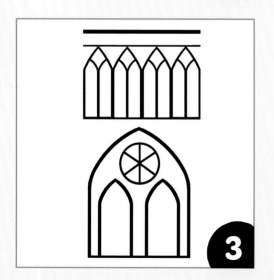

Step 2
Tape the cereal boxes together horizontally to make a large wall, as shown. Seal any openings with masking tape. Next, tape the two cracker box halves to the top of this wall. This is the basic facade of the cathedral.

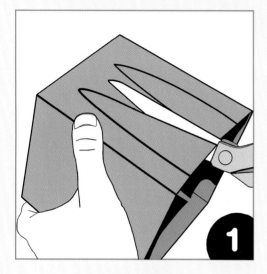

Step 3
Use the templates shown in this step as guides to cut archways out of scrap cardboard. Your measurements can be approximate, but they should be consistent across each side of the cathedral.

Step 4
Cut the archways out of cardboard with scissors. To make them more dimensional, layer the archways on top of each other, making them about 1/8 inch smaller

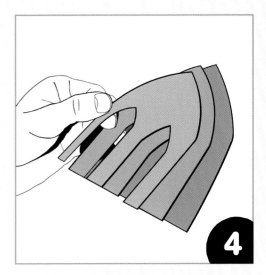

with each outer layer. Glue these archways to the first and second levels of your structure, as shown.

Step 5

Dip paper strips into glue and water mixture, and cover the entire structure with a layer of papier-mâché. Smooth away excess water and bubbles with a paintbrush. Allow time to dry. Cut out three to six of the smaller archways shown in the template in step 3 and glue them along the top of the second level. You may overlap these arches as necessary, depending on the width of your cathedral.

Step 6

Cut strips of cardboard to make several balconies. Glue in place. Add additional glued strips of cardboard to make other architectural details as desired. When finished, paint the entire cathedral with a sponge for a textured effect. Paint shadows with brushes around arches for a dramatic effect. Last, draw doorways, a rose window, and small circular windows using a compass and black felt tip marker.

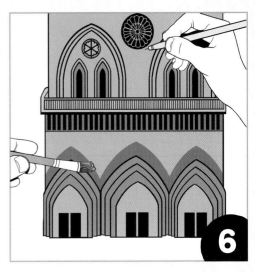

The Art of Decoration

Most everything inside a Gothic cathedral was symbolic. The importance of light had great meaning because it was the natural representation of God. To the millions of medieval worshippers, a visit to a cathedral was more than a way to show their devotion; it was also an entertaining destination, a place that housed great beauty in its sculptures, frescoes (wall paintings), holy relics, and stained glass windows.

The stained glass images were important. They were a way for the cathedral to convey to its parishioners that they should live more pious lifestyles. By examining the religious scenes depicted in stained glass, even the most illiterate people understood the importance of following Jesus's teachings, even if they could not read the Bible. The stained glass images were also remarkably beautiful. Who would not be in awe of bright sunlight streaming through colorful glass, especially since glass was so rare during the

In this medieval manuscript illumination, glassblowers practice their craft by blowing, twisting, and turning the hot glass as it cools. Glass was extremely rare and valuable during the Middle Ages.

Middle Ages? Twelfth-century chroniclers described England's redesigned Canterbury Cathedral as "a blaze of glass windows," while the famous stained glass windows at Chartres

Cathedral in France were known as *bleu de ciel*, or "heavenly blue." Many Gothic cathedrals of the Middle Ages featured circular rose windows, with patterns that were made to resemble the flower.

Glassmakers (or glaziers) often worked in the forests where the raw materials for their craft were located. The ash from beechwood trees was combined with sand and heated in a furnace, creating a chemical reaction. This process was called fritting. Afterward, the "frit" was blown through a long, iron tube to create a bubble that was cut and flattened. The process of adding color was also accomplished by specific chemical reactions, secret recipes that were handed down through the generations. Metallic oxides were often added to the molten glass to produce various colors: cobalt for blue, copper for red, iron for yellow, and so on. Glaziers then cut the colored glass and fit it together to recreate a sketch called a cartoon. The final pieces were sealed with lead and glass putty. The results were so well made that the lead would need to be replaced only once in a century.

The rose window in the north transept of Chartres Cathedral was assembled in the thirteenth century. Many European rose windows from the medieval period remain today since they were so well-built and maintained.

Many exquisite examples of medieval stained glass survive to this day. The windows of the Abbey Church of St. Denis in France are original, as are those in Chartres Cathedral and Le Mans. In England, visitors to York, Lincoln, and Salisbury cathedrals can enjoy stained glass from the medieval era.

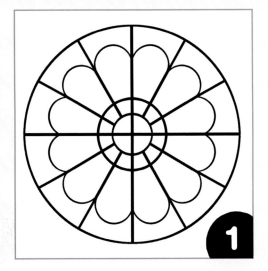

Stained Glass*

Traditional patterns help make this stained "glass" look like the real thing.
* ADULT SUPERVISION IS ADVISED FOR THIS CRAFT.

YOU WILL NEED

- Black oven-bake clay
- Hard candy in assorted colors
- Oven-proof glass pie plate
- Kitchen knife
- Baking sheet
- Parchment paper
- Hammer
- Toothpick
- Tweezers
- Plastic sandwich bags
- Paper and pencil or photocopied page

Step 1

Photocopy and enlarge this simple rose window design to approximately 5 inches in diameter. You can also draw your own design.

Step 2

To make the frame, place the paper design under your clear glass pie plate. Roll your black clay into long slender tubes. Beginning with the center cross, trace the image with the clay tubes using small pieces. Cut lines with your knife.

Step 3

Join the clay tubes together with the tip of a toothpick, and smooth the joints with your fingers. Make sure that the finished frame is fully joined.

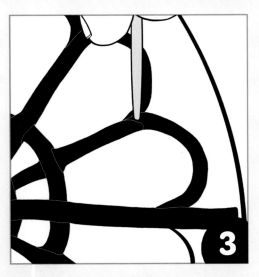

Step 4

Add a small band of clay at the top of the frame for hanging, as shown. After your clay foundation is complete, preheat your oven to the temperature indicated on the clay packaging instructions and bake the clay foundation. After baking, remove your clay from the oven and set it aside to cool. Next, gently remove it

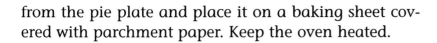

from the pie plate and place it on a baking sheet covered with parchment paper. Keep the oven heated.

Step 5

Sort your candies by color and place individual colored candies in separate sandwich bags. With a hammer, crush the candies into small pieces. It is not necessary to pound them into dust, but make them small.

Step 6

Fill the spaces within the frame with the crushed candy colors. Use tweezers or a toothpick to help guide the small pieces. Make sure that the spaces are thoroughly filled with candy. When finished, place the baking sheet in the oven and melt the candy for about two minutes. If there are open gaps within the spaces, fill them with more candy and return your craft to the oven for an additional 30 seconds to a minute.

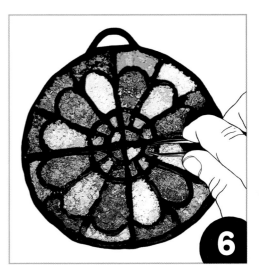

Sacred Imagery

Among the most profound religious images is that of Christ's crucifixion. This sacred image was found on many items during the Middle Ages, including wooden panel paintings, frescoes, enamel pendants, mosaics, stained glass, processional crosses, and metal, stone, ivory, and wood sculptures. Some items were even made with precious gemstones to revere the sacrifice that Christ made for mankind.

Sacred images were made to decorate church and cathedral interiors and castle and monastery chapels. They helped individuals remain focused on Christ's suffering and sacrifice. There was debate about the use of images becoming a form of idolatry. There was a risk that a person was worshipping the image of Jesus, not God. Nevertheless, people prayed to these images and believed that their prayers would be answered. Seeing Christ's image hanging on the cross

Pietro Cavallini painted this fresco of Christ on the cross during the thirteenth century. Sacred imagery took on a great role in medieval art, and frescoes (images painted directly onto wet plaster) remain among the most long-lasting images from the period.

and depicted in various media was a reminder of the belief in salvation in the afterlife. People looked to religious imagery for inspiration. They hoped

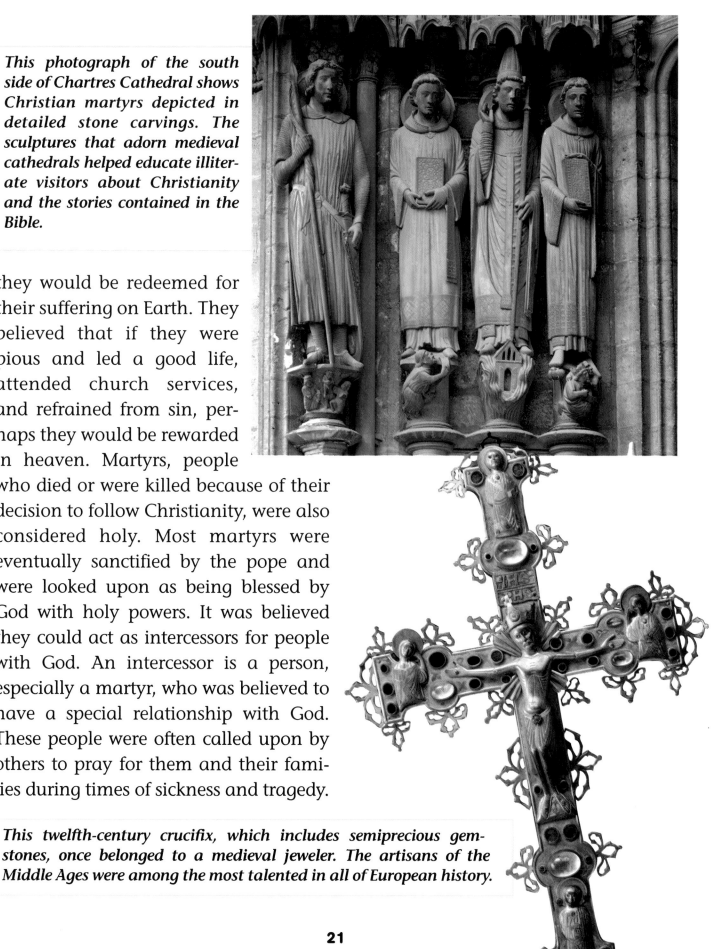

This photograph of the south side of Chartres Cathedral shows Christian martyrs depicted in detailed stone carvings. The sculptures that adorn medieval cathedrals helped educate illiterate visitors about Christianity and the stories contained in the Bible.

they would be redeemed for their suffering on Earth. They believed that if they were pious and led a good life, attended church services, and refrained from sin, perhaps they would be rewarded in heaven. Martyrs, people who died or were killed because of their decision to follow Christianity, were also considered holy. Most martyrs were eventually sanctified by the pope and were looked upon as being blessed by God with holy powers. It was believed they could act as intercessors for people with God. An intercessor is a person, especially a martyr, who was believed to have a special relationship with God. These people were often called upon by others to pray for them and their families during times of sickness and tragedy.

This twelfth-century crucifix, which includes semiprecious gemstones, once belonged to a medieval jeweler. The artisans of the Middle Ages were among the most talented in all of European history.

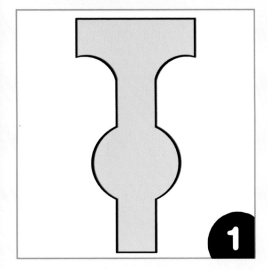

Iconic Cross*

Use found objects to create a traditional sacred cross like those that were popular during the late Middle Ages.
* ADULT SUPERVISION IS ADVISED FOR THIS CRAFT.

YOU WILL NEED
- Cardboard
- Manila folder (template)
- Oven-bake clay
- Discarded costume jewelry
- Assorted beads, various sizes
- Scissors
- Marker/pencil
- Glue
- String
- Pliers
- Toothpicks
- String
- Gold and light green/teal paint
- Brushes

Step 1
Enlarge the shape shown here and trace it onto a manila folder to make a template (pattern). The size of your template will dictate the size of your finished cross. Cut the template out.

Step 2
Use your template to repeatedly trace the design onto a large sheet of cardboard. The cardboard should be large enough so that you can repeat the design in the shape of a cross, roughly allowing for an extra inch or two to extend the cross's base farther than its arms. Your size relationships can be rough estimates. Once you are satisfied with your cross, cut it out and trace it onto another piece of cardboard to make an exact copy. Cut out the second cross and set it aside.

Step 3
Next, assemble your jewelry findings and/or pieces. Broken or mismatched earrings work well. Separate their parts with pliers. Carefully glue assorted pieces around the outer edge of one cross so that they all protrude

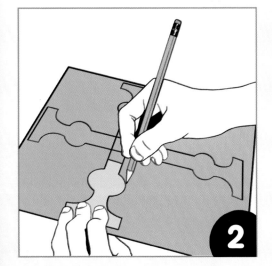

beyond its edge. When you are finished, glue the crosses together, concealing the areas where you just glued the jewelry. The jewelry, now sandwiched between two layers of cardboard, should be seen peering out from the outer edges of both crosses.

Step 4
To make the figures for the cross, make a variety of simple shapes from oven-bake clay. Follow package directions for baking. Set figures aside to cool.

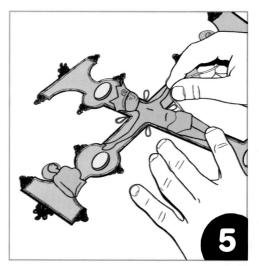

Step 5
Next, glue a single continuous strand of string along the cross's parameter. Use toothpicks to help guide the string if needed.

Step 6
Attach figures with glue. Allow time to dry. Paint entire cross, including figures, with gold paint. Allow more time to dry. Next, attach a variety of beads with glue. Highlight in light green/teal paint with a dry brush by softly going over areas that you want to emphasize.

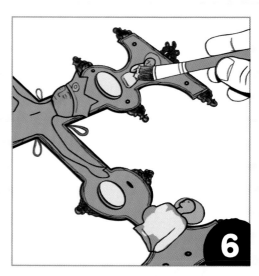

Cathedral Treasures

This thirteenth-century gemellion is made of enamel, gold, and copper, and is decorated with various creatures. Gemellions were used in pairs for washing hands during Mass. Water would stream out through the animal-head spout of one bowl into the other.

E ven the most modest cathedrals had their share of holy relics and treasures, some of which drew hundreds if not thousands of pilgrims every year. Many cathedrals were extremely wealthy, having for years received gifts of treasure from kings and merchants (much of which was pillaged from other churches and cathedrals). All cathedrals prized their treasury. Many items were kept on display in cupboards of the sacristy, where a treasurer (who slept there) could protect them. Other cathedrals kept valuable items locked away in underground crypts.

Larger cathedrals could afford to commission liturgy vessels (used for ceremonial rites), such as gold or silver chalices for wine (symbolizing the "blood" of Christ) and patens for bread (symbolizing the "body" of Christ). Alter crosses, candlesticks, enameled basins called gemellions (for washing), and cruets were just some of the exquisite treasures made for cathedral services by master craftsmen. Most of these treasures used imagery drawn from Christ's crucifixion, while others portrayed the apostles or the Virgin Mary. They were created using the most precious metals available, such as gold and silver. These treasures were then engraved with surprising detail. To further enhance their detail, their crevasses were often filled with niello, a hard compound of silver and sulfur, which helped contrast the brightly polished metals. Some also featured precious gems like amethysts and sapphires. When commissioning the treasures for the Abbey Church of St. Denis, Abbot Suger proclaimed, "If

This photograph shows a detail of a twelfth-century relic depicting Christ's crucifixion in gold, enamel, and precious and semiprecious gemstones. No expense was too great when creating holy relics and items used in traditional Catholic ceremonies.

golden pouring vessels serve to collect the blood of goats and calves, [then] how much more golden vessels, precious stones, and whatever is most valued . . . be laid out . . . for the reception of the blood of Christ!"

Still other treasures took a zoomorphic form, which means they took the shape of an animal. The most common zoomorphic form was that of a dove, which was used to hold the Communion wafer in the Eucharist—the Communion portion of Mass. (The Eucharist can also refer to the bread and wine symbolizing the body and blood of Jesus.) A hinged panel on the dove's back usually flipped open to reveal the Communion wafers inside. The dove is a symbol of the Holy Spirit, and it would normally hang high above the cathedral altar during Mass as a symbol of God's presence. Many Eucharist doves were made in France, where talented craftsmen in the city of Limoges were experts at creating liturgy treasures in precious metals with enamel inlays. Today, Limoges is still home to master craftsmen, only their contemporary specialty is working in porcelain.

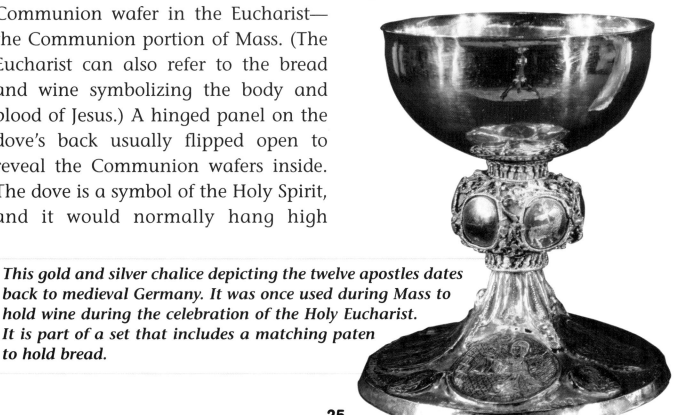

This gold and silver chalice depicting the twelve apostles dates back to medieval Germany. It was once used during Mass to hold wine during the celebration of the Holy Eucharist. It is part of a set that includes a matching paten to hold bread.

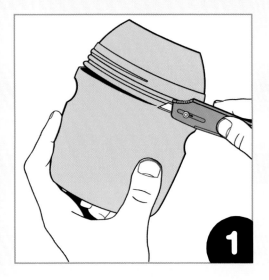

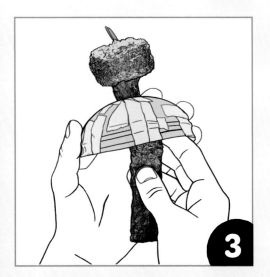

Chalice

Picture the wealth of your imaginary cathedral and the beautiful objects it held, such as this gorgeous golden chalice.

YOU WILL NEED

- Plastic powdered drink mix container
- Aluminum foil
- Paper fasteners
- Masking tape
- Awl
- Craft knife
- Scissors
- Glue
- String
- Gold paint
- Paintbrushes
- Bowl, glue/water mixture, and paper strips (for papier-mâché)

Step 1

Remove the top of your drink mix container. This is the chalice's vessel. Set it aside. Next, carefully cut the upper half of the interior drink mix container, as shown. Discard the rest, but keep both the interior top and the lid.

Step 2

With your scissors, make 1-inch cuts around the perimeter of the interior top's opening to create tabs. Overlap these tabs and tape them together with masking tape to narrow the opening. This will become the base of the chalice.

Step 3

The stem of the chalice is made from aluminum foil. Before you make this mushroom-shape with a long tail, poke a paper fastener through the foil and build the top of your mushroom around the fastener. Use a large piece of foil (at least two feet in length) and make your mushroom so it has a long tail, as shown. Insert the tail through the base of the chalice. Shape the tail into the chalice's stem, making it wider toward the bottom by wrapping the excess tail around one time.

Step 4

Take the outer lid of the drink mix container and make a hole in the center of its bottom with your awl. Push the paper fastener from the foil ball through the hole and attach the lid like a cup.

Step 5

Dip paper strips into glue and water mixture, and cover the entire chalice with several layers of papier-mâché. Smooth away excess water and bubbles with a paint-brush. Allow time to fully dry.

Step 6

Once dry, you can add detail by making a design with glue and setting pieces of string into it. Paint the entire chalice gold when finished.

Holy Sacraments

During the early Middle Ages, many sacraments shaped Christians' lives. The word "sacrament" comes from the Latin word *sacramentum*, which means "oath." It was translated from the Greek word for mystery *(musterion)* in the third century because Greeks referred to sacraments as mysteries. Sacraments are rituals in which God's grace is bestowed upon the participants. Many Christian rituals, such as baptism and receiving the Eucharist, have long been considered sacraments.

Like they did in the thirteenth century, today's Christians believe that there are seven sacraments. One of these sacraments, Holy Orders, is given only to those people who will go on to serve God in the cathedral or church. Most Christians today practice the other sacraments, including baptism, confirmation, marriage, receiving the Eucharist, confession, and the anointing of the sick, sometimes called last rites.

Confirmation is usually received after baptism and before marriage. It is

In this manuscript illumination, parents present their infant to be baptized. Baptism has been considered a holy sacrament since the medieval period. It remains among the seven sacraments that are today still practiced by many Christians.

seen as a reunion with the Holy Spirit and a reaffirmation of the sacrament of baptism. The first time a child receives the Eucharist is called his or her Holy Communion, after which Christians usually receive the Eucharist every Sunday, every holy day, and sometimes during the week.

Marriage is a unification of a man and woman. The sacrament of confession, though simple today, was quite complicated during the Middle Ages. Priests instructed from confessors' manuals that advised them how to ask questions during confession and to provide counsel without the mention of other sinful activities. Communication between priests and those who were confessing was highly formalized. The last sacrament, the anointing of the sick, was usually given to a person who was gravely ill. This was seen as a final way to absolve someone of sin before death. Today, priests are called on to perform last rites to a Christian person who is about to die.

A priest prays over a man of ill health in this medieval manuscript illumination that illustrates the Christian sacrament of anointing the sick. Since the time of the Middle Ages, priests offer blessings and spiritual peace to those who have fallen seriously ill by anointing their hands and forehead with holy oil.

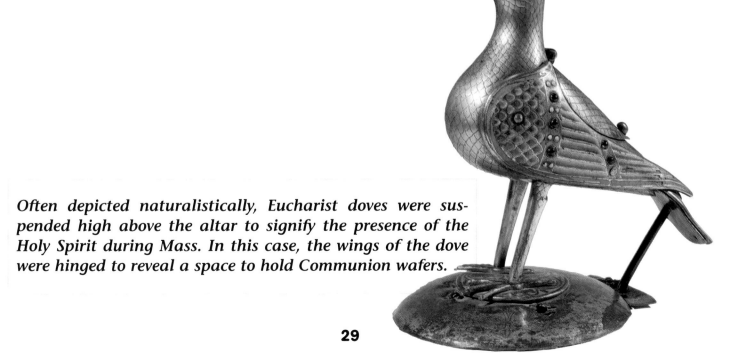

Often depicted naturalistically, Eucharist doves were suspended high above the altar to signify the presence of the Holy Spirit during Mass. In this case, the wings of the dove were hinged to reveal a space to hold Communion wafers.

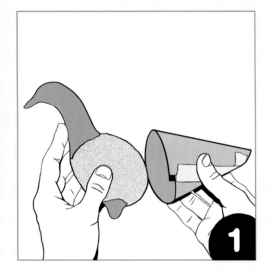

Eucharist Dove

Symbolizing the Holy Spirit, the Eucharist dove rested high above the cathedral altar.

YOU WILL NEED

- Modeling clay
- Styrofoam egg
- Cardboard
- Pencil
- Masking tape
- Glue
- Craft knife
- Scissors
- String
- Paper fasteners
- Straight pins
- 2 bamboo skewers
- Paint
- Paintbrush
- Bowl, glue/water mixture, and paper strips (for papier-mâché)
- Awl

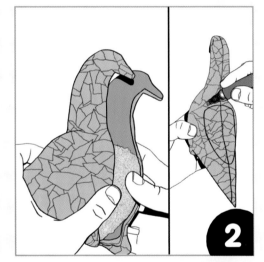

Step 1

Begin with a Styrofoam egg, which will be the dove's body. With modeling clay, sculpt a head and neck by rolling clay into a tube shape and bending it into an arc. Pinch the top end of the arc to make the dove's beak. Attach this shape to the Styrofoam. Add two balls of clay to make the dove's thighs. Roll a piece of cardboard into a cone to make the dove's tail. Tape the cone shut. Attach the cone with straight pins. Dip paper strips into glue and water mixture, and cover the entire surface of the dove with 3 to 4 layers of papier-mâché. Smooth away excess water and bubbles with a paintbrush. Allow time to fully dry.

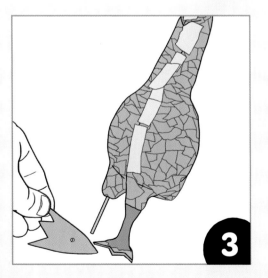

Step 2

With your craft knife, carefully cut through the center of the dove, creating two halves. Remove the egg and scoop out the clay. Hold the two halves back together. Draw an oval shape on the dove's back, as shown, and cut it out from both sides with scissors.

Step 3

Tape the halves back together with masking tape. Insert a bamboo skewer into each of the "thighs," and let the

skewers go up into the dove's head. You can hold the skewers in place on the hollow inside with a bit of clay. To make the feet, cut two 3-inch triangles from cardboard and make a hole in each. Glue the ends of the skewers into the holes. Build the legs up with clay.

Step 4

Add a small ball of clay to the top of the opening cut in the dove's back. Pinch it to form a lip. Cover the entire bird with papier-mâché and set aside to dry.

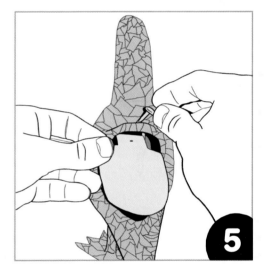

Step 5

Cut a piece of cardboard that is somewhat larger than the oval-shaped opening in the dove's back. Make it so it has a square shape at the top, as shown. Bend the cardboard so that it fits well. With an awl, make a hole in the center of this square and a hole through the lip of the opening. Join together with a paper fastener.

Step 6

Draw wings and eyes on your dove. Trace the lines with glued pieces of string. When fully dry, paint the dove as you desire.

A Traditional Mass

This medieval Christian altar depicts the seven sacraments. Many Christian rituals were re-created in works of art in order to teach people morality and to keep Christianity ever-present in peoples' lives and hearts.

During the Middle Ages, cathedral services were held in Latin, but the sermons were spoken in English since Latin was the language of the educated. As mentioned before, most people could not read or write, so they could not follow along or respond to a priest in mass. It is for this reason that the visual elements of the cathedrals were so important. When people could not understand the ceremony, they could be instructed instead by images in stained glass, mosaics, panel paintings and triptychs (three-paneled paintings), and sculptures. When stained glass windows were implemented in most cathedrals, their images were used as teaching devices. Dramatic storytelling was also used to teach morality and raise awareness of correct behavior. Anecdotes of moral lessons were called exempla. Priests conducted five services each day of the week except on Sundays, the Christian holy day, when seven services took place.

Unlike the formality of today's services, little about medieval masses was consistent. Priests, though they were educated, basically conducted services in their individual way, some of them telling dramatic tales about the hellfire that awaited sinners. Music

This hand-carved ivory book cover from the court of ninth-century King Charles of France shows a Christian Mass in progress. Detailed carvings in ivory were among the most exquisite art works from the medieval period in European art.

and singing were usually a large part of the service, especially in cathedrals, which had wonderful acoustics. As it was in monasteries, this singing usually took the form of chanting, often of specific psalms. Priests did have some formality when distributing Communion: washing in the altar basin, pouring the wine and drinking from the chalice, and eating the Communion wafer. Most every other part of the Mass was unique. Some priests would recount local crimes and losses, while others would use the service as a way to unite the community.

Some priests worked outside of the cathedral as well. In England, priests conducted short services outside of the church in small chapels called chantries, where they were paid a small sum to hold a service for those who had died.

This ornate censer depicting a Gothic motif was created around 1450. Medieval priests used censers to burn incense during Mass, yet another way to inspire parishioners' senses.

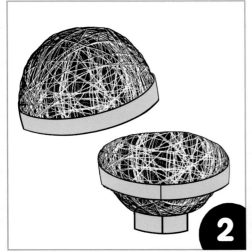

Incense Censer

Medieval priests swung censers like this one filled with incense to purify the air during Mass. You can use this censer to purify the air in your home by filling it with sweet-smelling herbs or potpourri.

YOU WILL NEED

- **White glue**
- **String**
- **2 small balloons**
- **Bowl**
- **Cardboard**
- **Scissors**
- **Awl**
- **Craft knife**
- **Ruler**
- **Gold paint**
- **Paintbrush**

Step 1

Blow up one balloon to the size of a small grapefruit and the other to the size of an egg. Knot them both. Pour white glue into a small bowl. With your hands, coat string in the glue. Wind the string around each balloon separately. Wrap the string vertically, then horizontally, then any which way until you have a nice web design. Set both balloons aside to dry.

Step 2

After the glue has dried and the string has hardened, pop the balloons with your awl and pull out the excess rubber. Set the smaller ball aside. With scissors, cut the large ball into two bowl-shaped pieces so that the top half is larger than the bottom. Cut two strips of cardboard, about 1 inch in width and with a length that completely wraps around the rim of both halves. Glue them to the rims, as shown. Cut another length of cardboard and glue it into a band on the bottom of the smaller half. This will be the censer's stand.

Step 3

When the cardboard strips have dried, put both halves of the ball shape back together. To hinge them, take your awl and carefully make four holes in the cardboard: two along the bottom edge of the top half, and two matching holes along the top edge of the bottom half, as shown. Insert a length of string through these holes and tie them together.

Step 4

To make a clasp for the front of your censer, make a hole in both the upper and lower strips as you did in step 3. Cut a small piece of cardboard in the shape of a number 7 and glue it into the bottom hole, as shown. Knot a piece of string into a loop, and glue the knot inside the top hole. Push the string in with your awl. Adjust the length of your loop so that it can snuggly fit over the bottom 7.

Step 5

Cut another band of cardboard to fit around the smaller ball to make the top. Cut out a cross from cardboard and glue it to the top. Glue the smaller ball to the top center of your large ball.

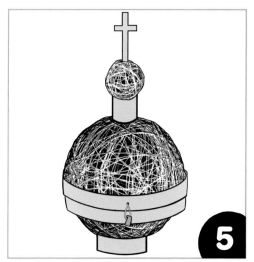

Step 6

Once the censer has dried, tie a 25-inch piece of string to its bottom left and bottom right sides. Tie another piece of string, roughly 14 inches in length, to the top just behind the cross. Tie these three pieces of string together at the top.

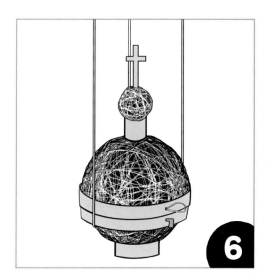

Remains of a Spiritual Past

Most cathedrals at one time or another housed spiritual relics. These were the remains of a holy site or holy person such as a saint contained in ornate, decorated boxes called reliquary caskets or, more plainly, reliquaries. Sometimes reliquaries took the shape of a body part (when a holy person's body part was housed inside). In other cases, the reliquary was a bust resembling the saint whose personal items—or whose skull—were contained inside. Today, most of the reliquaries are works of art without any interior contents. During the Middle Ages, reliquaries were often displayed on the cathedral altar or carried in procession.

Cathedrals sought to have a variety of relics and other valuables in their treasury. Keeping these items ensured steady visits from pilgrims and frequent donations to their coffers. The holiest and most desirable relics were associated with Christ and the Virgin Mary. These items were cherished and protected, and people often risked their

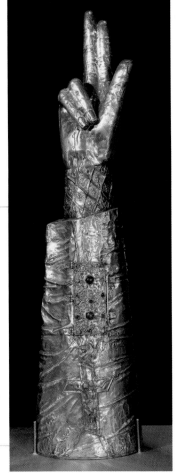

The Arm of Saint George is a medieval reliquary that dates back to the ninth century. It once held the remains of a monk who rose to become a bishop in 877. Saint George is the patron saint of England.

lives to save them from fire and theft. When Vikings and other so-called barbarian groups raided churches and monasteries during the early Middle Ages, priests and monks ran into the forests carrying these "caskets" in the hopes of protecting the items inside.

Kings and other nobles often passed holy relics into the hands of bishops for safekeeping. Charles the Bald, grandson of King Charlemagne, reportedly gave a piece of a cloak worn by the Virgin Mary to the bishop of Chartres Cathedral in 876. In the years that followed, thousands made a pilgrimage to Chartres to see a glimpse of the fabric.

This photograph shows the reliquary of the True Cross in silver, gold, enamel, and gemstones. It remains one of the richest and most elaborate containers from the Middle Ages.

Other cathedrals claimed to have strands of the Virgin Mary's hair, pieces of her veil, or a tiny vial of her breast milk.

An entire cult of pilgrims reportedly visited Chartres and other places where relics associated with the Virgin Mary were housed. Many of these pilgrims believed in the healing properties associated with the relics, and some even claimed to have been healed by them.

Other popular relics were associated with the crucifixion of Jesus Christ and claimed to be a part of the True Cross. Many of these items were reported to be nails and shards of wood from the cross on which Jesus died, though most were likely ordinary wood scraps. Among the most famous relics is the Holy Grail, a vessel said to have been used by Jesus during the Last Supper. It is also thought to be the vessel that caught Jesus's blood when he was pierced by a soldier's sword as he hung on the cross. Though it has never been found, pilgrims have been hunting for it since the Middle Ages.

This small French reliquary in gold-plated silver, pearls, and precious gemstones likely contained the remains of a monk. It dates back to the eighth century.

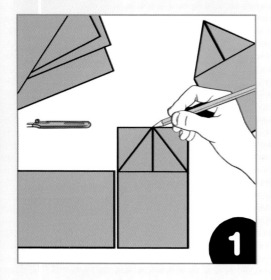

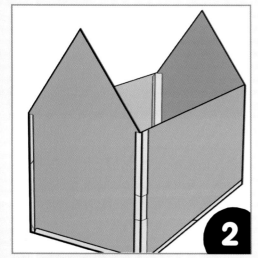

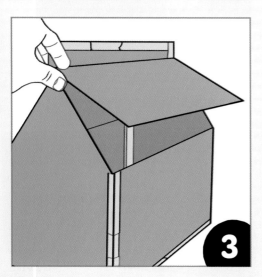

Reliquary Casket

Sacred objects like fragments of fabric and the bones of saints were stored in fine decorated cabinets and displayed inside cathedrals. What will you store inside your reliquary casket?

YOU WILL NEED

- Cardboard
- Ruler and pencil
- Craft knife
- Scissors
- Masking tape
- Gold foil doiles
- Plastic craft jewels or found objects
- Paint
- Paintbrush
- Acrylic gloss medium
- Gold cord or fabric trim

Step 1

Cut five 11-by-6-inch rectangles from cardboard—one each for the lid, top, front, back, and bottom of your casket. Cut two 9 1/2-by-6-inch pieces for the sides, and four 1 1/2-by-6-inch pieces for the feet. Take two of the 9 1/2-inch pieces and draw a line with a ruler and pencil making the bottom part of each one into a 6-inch square. Mark the top of both pieces at the middle (3 inches). Next, draw two diagonal lines from the top of the pieces to the corner of the square, forming triangles. Cut away the excess, making pointed side walls.

Step 2

Tape the two pointed side walls to two of the 11-by-6-inch pieces, forming a box. Tape an additional piece for the bottom.

Step 3

Take the two remaining large pieces, and with your craft knife and ruler, score the cardboard 1 inch from the long edge. With the scored edge at the top, tape one of the boards to the back and sides of the casket, folding the

38

scored edge so it bends upward, as shown. Next, tape the scored edge of the second board to the top of the first one to make a top that opens.

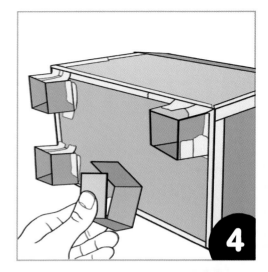

Step 4
Next, take the 1 1/2-by-6-inch pieces, and fold them every 1 1/2 inches to make cubes. Tape them closed. Tape the cubes to the bottom of the casket. Once your casket is fully assembled, paint it a solid color.

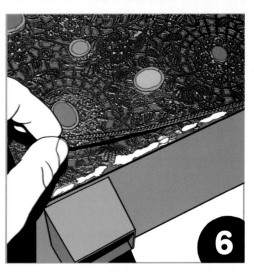

Step 5
Cover the entire surface of the casket with cut doily pieces using a brush and acrylic gloss medium. Allow time to dry.

Step 6
Glue craft gems, beads, or found objects to the surface. Cut pieces of gold cord to fit the length and width of the casket sides and glue them around the edges to dress them up. You can also glue gold string around the "gems" for added detail, or glue a photograph of you or your family in the center.

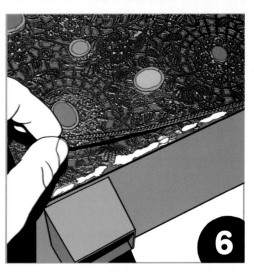

A Spiritual Journey

In this manuscript illumination, a group of men in Canterbury, England, are heading out on a pilgrimage. Long-distance journeys became more and more popular during the Middle Ages, especially as word about the magnificent cathedrals spread from city to city.

T he act of going on a pilgrimage, traveling to a sacred place to pay one's respects, became popular during the late Middle Ages. This was especially true during the rise of cathedral building. In fact, when news spread of the awesome, beautiful structures that were being built throughout western Europe, people of all ages wanted to visit them in person.

Although traveling was difficult, Christians made journeys to local shrines, sacred places where saints had lived, had worked, or were buried. Christians made pilgrimages to be forgiven if they sinned or to be cured of illness. The most sacred places of all were the Holy Lands of the East, cities such as Jerusalem, though few medieval Christians could travel so far.

In England, the most popular shrine was the tomb of Thomas Becket at Canterbury Cathedral. Medieval English writer Geoffrey Chaucer wrote expressively about the act of Christian pilgrimage to this site in his famous work *The Canterbury Tales*. This work was a collection of stories of pilgrims and their travels. In one story, he remarked how Christians spoke rather glamorously of their journeys, pointing out the fact that many of them had exaggerated their experiences: ". . . men and women be a monethe out in their pilgrimage, many of them shall be, [a] halfe yeare after, great janglers, taletellers, and lyers . . ." But surely not all Christians' stories of happenings along their wanderings were untrue. After all, medieval travelers encountered plenty on their journeys, including merchants and traders carrying luxury

goods, and spent nights in the company of monks, taking their meals in silence and sleeping in foreign monasteries.

Specific relics—articles of fabric, bones, and pieces of wood said to have touched Jesus or Mary—also drew many pilgrims. Cathedrals often had their items on display or enshrined so visitors could get as close as possible to the sacred items. Pilgrims collected lead badges, called pilgrim badges, which they sewed to their hats as an indication or remembrance of the sites they had visited. Certainly the act of pilgrimage led to a new sense of knowledge and awareness during the medieval period. This knowledge of a larger world and of cultures and ideas not native to the pilgrims', was just one spark that would eventually ignite the Renaissance, or rebirth, of knowledge in the coming centuries.

Pilgrim Badge*

Pretend that you are traveling to a cathedral in a holy city to visit the shrine of a Christian saint. To remember your journey, you might wear a pilgrim badge as a sign of your devotion.
* ADULT SUPERVISION IS ADVISED FOR THIS CRAFT.

YOU WILL NEED
- **Paper and pencil or photocopied page**
- **Aluminum foil baking pan**
- **Ballpoint pen**
- **Pencil**
- **Masking tape**
- **Glue stick**
- **Scissors**
- **Lightweight cardboard (like a cereal box)**
- **Black craft paint and brush**
- **Safety pin**
- **Tweezers**
- **Protective gloves**

Step 1
Photocopy and enlarge this badge design to 6 inches in height. You can also draw your own design. Whichever method you choose, cut the picture out.

Step 2
Cut out the bottom of a foil baking pan with scissors. Discard the sides. Be careful, the edges are sharp. Cut the metal into a rectangle that is slightly larger than your badge design. Tape the paper to the foil. To emboss the metal, place the foil onto a piece of cardboard. With a ballpoint pen, firmly trace the design into the foil. Flip the foil over to see the embossed image on the reverse side.

Step 3
After the image is traced into the foil, remove the paper. With scissors, cut the foil badge out, leaving a 1/8-inch border. Use care when handling sharp edges, or wear gloves.

Step 4

Set the badge onto your cardboard work surface, indented side up. With your pen, fill the horse's body with clusters of dots. Apply stronger pressure to areas you want to raise on the reverse side. Use a pencil to emboss the figure, coloring in his features.

Step 5

Take the paper image you used to trace and glue it to the cardboard with a glue stick. Cut the design out, cutting within the outer line so that it is slightly smaller than your metal version. With scissors, cut tabs around the metal badge and fold them over onto the cardboard.

Step 6

To add detail to your embossing, cover the front of the badge with black paint. With your fingertip, gently wipe off the paint from the surface while leaving paint in the crevasses.

TIMELINE

A.D.   **313**   Constantine imposes the Edict of Milan, preaching tolerance for Christianity.

410   Visigoths sack Rome.

circa 476   The Roman Empire falls.

476–1000   The period historians sometimes refer to as Europe's Dark Ages.

circa 700   Feudal system is established in France.

711   Muslims invade Spain.

768   Charlemagne becomes king of the Franks.

793   Beginning of Viking raids in England.

1066   William the Conqueror conquers England.

1095   Pope Urban II urges Christian knights to defend Christianity.

1096–1291   The Christian Crusades are launched to recapture the Holy Land from Muslims.

1161   First guilds are established; the era of cathedral building begins.

1171   The Bank of Venice opens.

1179   The third Lateran Council decrees all cathedrals must have schools.

1180   Windmills first appear in Europe.

1215   The fourth Lateran Council requires Jews to wear identifying badges; signing of the Magna Carta.

1241   Mongols invade Europe.

1271   Marco Polo travels to Asia.

1300   Feudalism ends.

1314–1322   The great famine (alternate droughts and heavy rains in northern Europe).

1337–1453   Hundred Years' War between England and France.

1347–1530   The plague kills about 25 million people throughout Europe.

1381   Peasants Revolt.

1453   The fall of Constantinople to Ottoman Turks (often taken as end of Middle Ages).

GLOSSARY

apse The rounded end of a cathedral.

arcade A row of arches used to support a roof.

basilica A Christian church with a rounded eastern end.

bishop A powerful church official whose job it was to oversee a diocese.

buttress A stone mass positioned at points of stress to support roofs, arches, or vaults.

chapel A separate area for worship, with its own altar, in a cathedral.

choir The area in the apse of a church reserved for the clergy.

Christianity The religion derived from the teachings of Jesus Christ.

coffer A chest or treasury for storing valuables.

cross vault (groin vault) Two half cylinders of stone that intersect at right angles.

cruciform Cross-shaped; the typical design of a medieval cathedral with transepts on the northern and southern points.

Crusades Religious wars fought between Christians and Muslims between 1096 and 1291.

crypt The underground area beneath a cathedral.

finial A miniature spire.

flying buttress A stone pier on the outside of a church connected by an arch that provides extra support for high cathedral walls.

Gothic An architectural period (1150–1400) whose style was dominated by pointed windows called lancets, high vaulted ceilings, and flying buttresses.

nave The long, main part of a cathedral that runs from east to west.

plague A deadly disease that came into Europe in 1347.

relic A sacred object that once belonged to a saint or to Jesus.

rib vault In Gothic architecture, a vault with bands of projecting stonework along the angles.

Romanesque An architectural period (900–1200) whose style is known for rounded columns and rounded arches.

transept The part of the cathedral that runs from north to south and that crosses the nave of a cruciform structure.

FOR MORE INFORMATION

The Metropolitan Museum of Art
1000 Fifth Avenue
New York, NY 10028-0198
(212) 535-7710
Web site: http://www.metmuseum.org

Washington National Cathedral
Massachusetts and Wisconsin
    Avenues NW
Washington, DC 20016-5098

(202) 537-6263
Web site: http://www.cathedral.org

WEB SITES

Due to the changing nature of Internet links, the Rosen Publishing Group, Inc., has developed an online list of Web sites related to the subject of this book. This site is updated regularly. Please use this link to access the list:

http://www.rosenlinks.com/ccma/meca

FOR FURTHER READING

AvRutick, Sharon, ed. *Cathedrals and Castles: Building in the Middle Ages* (Discoveries). New York, NY: Harry N. Abrams, Inc., 1995.

Gies, Francis, and Joseph Gies. *Cathedral, Forge, and Waterwheel: Technology and Invention in the Middle Ages*. New York, NY: HarperCollins Publishers, 1995.

Hilliam, David. *Castles and Cathedrals: The Great Buildings of Medieval Times* (The Library of the Middle Ages). New York, NY: The Rosen Publishing Group, 2004.

Macaulay, David. *Cathedral: The Story of Its Construction*. New York, NY: Houghton Mifflin/Walter Lorrain Books, 1981.

MacDonald, Fiona. *A Medieval Cathedral* (Inside Story). New York, NY: Peter Bendick, 2001.

INDEX

ABOUT THE AUTHOR/ILLUSTRATOR

In the past, Joann Jovinelly and Jason Netelkos have collaborated on many educational projects for young people. This is their second crafts series that encourages youngsters to learn history through hands-on projects. Their first series, Crafts of the Ancient World, was published by the Rosen Publishing Group in 2001. They live in New York City.

PHOTO CREDITS

Cover (center), pp. 21 (top), 25 (top), 29 (bottom), 32, 36, 37 (bottom) Erich Lessing/ Art Resource, NY; p. 4 © Walter Bibikow/Index Stock Imagery, Inc; p. 5 Courtesy of the University of Texas Libraries, The University of Texas at Austin; p. 7 © Craig Lovell/ Corbis; p. 9 © Patrick Ward/Corbis; p. 10 Permission British Library (Royal 16 G. VI); p. 11 The Granger Collection, New York; p. 12 © The British Library/HIP/The Image Works; p. 13 (top) © Adam Woolfitt/Corbis; p. 13 (bottom) © Artifice, Inc./ GreatBuildings.com; pp. 16, 40 British Library, London, UK/Bridgeman Art Library; p. 17 © Angelo Hornak/Corbis; p. 20 © Mimmo Jodice/Corbis; p. 21 (bottom) © Elio Ciol/ Corbis; p. 24 © The British Museum/Topham-HIP/The Image Works; p. 25 (bottom) Scala/Art Resource, NY; p. 28 Permission British Library (Royal 6 E. VI); p. 29 (top) Permission British Library (Royal 6 E. VII); p. 33 (top) Réunion des Musées Nationaux/ Art Resource, NY; p. 33 (bottom) © Leonid Bogdanov/SuperStock; p. 37 (top) Werner Foreman/Art Resource, NY; p. 41 (top) Nimatallah/Art Resource, NY; p. 41 (bottom) © Museum of London, UK/Bridgeman Art Library. All crafts designed by Jason Netelkos and Joann Jovinelly. All craft illustrations by Jason Netelkos. All craft photography by Joann Jovinelly.

Special thanks to Christina Burfield for her continued support and encouragement.

Designer: Evelyn Horovicz; Editor: Leigh Ann Cobb
Photo Researcher: Gabriel Caplan